CUSTOMERS

Yvonne Trainer

Acknowledgements:- some of these poems have appeared in *Black Willow Poetry, Contemporary Verse II, Junction, Poetry Toronto, Student Oracle, Watchwords, West Coast Review and Whetstone;* some have been read on CBC Anthology.

Published by Fiddlehead Poetry Books, Fredericton, New Brunswick, Canada, with the assistance of the Canada Council, the New Brunswick Department of Cultural and Historical Resources, and the University of New Brunswick.

©Yvonne Trainer, 1983

Cover design by Alexander McGibbon

Dedication: for my Grandfather, Claude Trainer (1902-1979); also for my good friend and mentor, Martin Oordt.

Canadian Cataloguing in Publication Data

Trainer, Yvonne.
  Customers

Poems.
ISBN 0-86492-036-9

I. Title.

PS8589.R34C87   C811'.54   C83-098274-4
PR9199.3.T72C87

CONTENTS
(by first lines)

Fingers Small and Brittle

We're at the Market Square	7
The waiter is crippled	9
"Green matches"	10
They lean over the bargain counter exclaiming	11
This is my last night	12
Autumn wind takes over	13
This trucker comes in	14
GREEN LETTUCE AND YELLOW CORN GONE	15
Are those the Muses	16

Elbow to Elbow

Restless all night	18
My old shoes stand empty	19
In fancy dress shops	20
The man in the white lab coat	21
Can it be memory	22
Buying gifts for literary friends	23
Shopping carts clash in mid-afternoon	24
I tell Mr. Lam Tam	25
At a craft shop an ancient man	26
Like a fish	27
In an instant	28
Who bought these?	29
At the shopping mall a Boy Scout	30
"There is no fun in anything"	31
Remembering how we moved closer together	32
In the doorway	33
A lantern swings light	34
You are crying	35
There are no pockets in this city	36
Expensive wine and a place to dine	37
Getting your children	38
I am reading about death	39
The owner of this shop	40
Where is that sound?	41
There is poetry in his action	42
His mother has a face like a bird	43

I pass a red ticket 44
Yesterday I got contact lenses 45
I am a consumer of medicare 46
They have closed the doors on the dead 47
Sometimes she gets happy 48
They never took pictures 49
Summer descends on the city 50
Air Canada has taken my luggage 51
What should I carry into this day? 52

* * *

Fingers Small and Brittle

We're at the Market Square
Mother buys cucumbers and lettuce
She holds my hand
points with the other
to the ripe tomatoes
(We're in a hurry
My Father is waiting)
She asks for five pounds
Five is the age I am

I don't like the Market Square
Kids with black hair and black eyes
stare around the sides
of fat Chinaman mothers
Groups of old women talk funny
They make noises in their throats
My Mother says they speak Russian
I'm afraid

I want to hide in the big basket
of green and yellow corn
but Mother is still clutching my hand
and pointing to the tomatoes
to make the lady understand
she only wants ripe ones
"Stupid Chinaman lady   You'd think she'd know
my Father will only eat ripe tomatoes"

I'm afraid
The old women laugh louder
They swing their long dresses like crazy
They finger the lettuce
I beg to go
I remind my Mother that Father will be angry
She only says "Aren't the pumpkins lovely"?
I'm quick to reply "They're ugly"
while the Chinaman lady puts her thumb on the scale

When we leave
Mother lets me carry a sack
We must walk past the old women
I clutch the bag with both fists
My Mother threatens to take it away
"Stop that" she snaps
"You'll squash them"

At supper my Father eats tomatoes
Two bites for each one
and a pound of salt
Smacking his lips
he lets the juice mix
with the snuff
at the corners of his mouth
Wiping his hands on dirty workpants
he curses the forecast of an early Fall

Talks long and loud of war
somewhere across the ocean

I beg to be excused.

*   *   *

The waiter is crippled:
big head
two shrunken legs
fingers   small and brittle
as chicken bones

"I don't want to eat here"
I whisper
but my Father is buttering his bread
My Mother is sipping her tea

When the meal comes
I refuse to taste it
My Mother tries to make me
My Father says "You're ill"

But after my Father eats both meals
Leaves a tip
and pays the bill
the waiter hands me two licorice-sticks
as twisted as his legs

I eat them
on the way home.

* * *

"Green matches"

He looks at me
I put a penny on the counter

He opens a packet
strikes a match
Its flame dances green

I laugh
I've never seen
a green flame

He holds it high
It reaches his fingers

"Blow it out" I plead
but he lets it burn

His finger-tips blister
white and sore
then red

The flame dies

He strikes another
Holds it high

I run
crying.

* * *

They lean over the bargain counter exclaiming
They hold silk slips to big bellies   They wear
soft skin against soft cloth   My Mother holds up a brassiere
and the white cups sag

A man in a blue suit announces sales
My Father leans one arm across a rack of dresses
I am interested in the rows of bicycle tires
the many rubber smells

The shelves are packed with linen   straw hats
boxes of socks   "This might fit you"
Mother says   "This might"

I am exposed   I may as well be etched
in white glow paint   "Get in there"
she says   "And try this"
Every stuffed animal ear turns to look

Though I am silent and never talk back   I see my Father
putting his third finger to his thumb
It snaps against my skull like strong elastic
"Listen to your Mother" he says.

*   *   *

This is my last night
in this bed   This is where
I slept with bubble gum in my mouth
got it stuck in my hair   I wore this hole
in the mattress   These are
my new suitcases
by the door   looking like
our family   Large to small
Father   Mother   daughter

and the overnight case
well   it's not new
but it isn't used
I was never invited
They never went far.

*   *   *

Autumn wind takes over
a hand slamming a door
on the pains of the day
the Apple man accepts it
he's used to wind
blowing in branches of trees

Now in this town
under a house of sky
with a truck full of fruit
he tacks up signs
to show the price
of apples
swollen and bruised
as the ankles
of fat old women

He sways with the wind
looking out
from under raised brows
he clutches his hat
in one hand
juggles apples
with the other

Not one customer.

* * *

This trucker comes in
cold as night   I say
"Sir   nice truck you've got"
He glares   I say
"Bet you work for Irvin"   He says
"Give me ten bucks worth of gas"

I squeeze the lever
The numbers click
It runs a nickel over
I spill some on my blouse

"OK"   I say
He says
"Got a place
where a guy
can take a leak"?

I say
"It's locked
I'll get the key"
He says
"That's OK"
and stands against the wheel

It happens often

Makes me madder
than hell
Boss always blamin' me
for spillin'
more than I do.

*   *   *

GREEN LETTUCE AND YELLOW CORN GONE
THE TURNIPS SOLD   AND THE WRINKLED CHINAMAN
THE WRINKLED CHINAMAN DRIVING AWAY
EMPTY BASKETS IN AN EMPTY TRUCK
THE RUSTY ENDGATE DOWN
RATTLES   NOT GOODBYE TO PHOEBE
BUT GOODBYE TO EMPTY STALLS
AND BOARDS NAILED OVER WINDOWS

PHOEBE WILL NOT SEE AGAIN   YET SHE STAYS
THE LAST PERSON ON THE WOODEN BENCH
THE LAST SHADOW ON THE SIDEWALK
HER HEAD IS FULL NOW WITH SOUNDS OF MAGPIES
PECKING BITS OF STRAW
BITS OF STRAW   THE MAGPIES PECKING.

* * *

Are those the Muses
singing? Cut Medusa's head
Blood flares into open sky

Is that Pegasus
being sold? A poet dreams
with cold hands in his pockets

Could that be a youth
stepping forth? A kingly beast
unfolds a splendour of wings.

* * *

Elbow To Elbow

Restless all night
Birds feather mad
in dark bush
The drunkard in room thirteen
trips ten steps to the bathroom

Awake in a rented bed
I find cigarette holes
in the sheets
with bare toes

Shadows
make me throw covers off
pace to the street-lit window
and back

also curve the east sun
bring it close
filter it through
the fly-specked screen.

* * *

My old shoes stand empty
I tuck toes into new pumps
tighten straps around heels
The shop assistant watches

She knows my size   the type of sole
the way I walk   Like a bloodhound
she could track me anywhere

When I leave
I will wear my shoes
on the other feet.

* * *

In fancy dress shops
my words
stiffen like ruffles
become as thick as drapes

no defense
against the pompous ladies
in flowered dresses
who insist

In fitting rooms
no choice
but to expose
   feet
      ankles
         legs

I always act quickly
Hang the dresses
on silver hooks
take off my shoes
roll my pantlegs to the knees
and wait.

* * *

The man in the white lab coat
sees everything I buy
He pretends not to
but how can he help it
when he checks prices
and puts things in bags?

Mostly I buy Q-tips
and eye-drops   Once
every few years a new
hot water bottle

Yet always
I feel his thoughts
settling like undissolved pills
in glasses of still water

Who knows the lump
in this man's head or stomach
How big it is
How large it might grow?

* * *

Can it be memory
that throws a shadow
on this hour?

Just past Carnellie's
Sporting Goods
I think of all those guns
pointed in the direction
of the mounted heads
Of hooks
ready to be baited
and cast out
into Summer waters

I turn to the park
where deer graze
A bird whistles
Among trees
a woman
carves words inches deep
into wood
that will not heal

Better not to think
when walking
Better just to walk
with the birdwatchers
looking for bright flickers
in high branches
or to stroll along the river
with the vacationers
Always in the shadows
singing to a shadow.

* * *

Buying gifts for literary friends
my hands grasp an urn
A Grecian urn

Yet on it one picture missing
Could it be the sacrifice?
It is the sacrifice

How can I give a Grecian urn
without the offering?
I cannot give an urn
without an offering

Better to keep it
to grow a red geranium in.

* * *

Shopping carts clash in mid-
afternoon   I reach for the ham
See month-old twins
wrapped like pink turkeys
in her basket

Cold air from the meat stand
freezes my tongue

She compliments the colors
of my blouse
Expects me
to praise her daughters
in return

I chortle at them
They wave small hands
Wings I think *Wings*
"Angels" I say
              "Angels"!

* * *

I tell Mr. Lam Tam
he'll need a parka
to wear to work
He looks at me blankly
I repeat *parka*
coat   jacket
Even these words
do not reach

I say
mitts   boots   cap
He looks at me strangely
In the hour before snow
I repeat the words
for him
for his wife
for his children

I usher them
to the downtown Mall
They stand
silent   stiff
The whole family
holding hands
while I dress them
like paper dolls.

* * *

At a craft shop an ancient man
carves tiny ships out of bone

The professor on leave sends cards
from the Atlantic to his family

On the corner a one-legged sailor
curses the pain of a phantom limb

The child's eye watches the vessel
that sails away from the shore

I eat white fish with pink sauce
and pretend that it is lobster.

* * *

Like a fish
it has fins
and a tail

It is fleshy-pink
to greenish-grey

Its head is slick
and its body
scaly

It is in an aquarium
of its own
Though it is for sale
no one goes near

When I tap the glass
it blows smoke
out of its nostrils
and hides in the plastic
seaweed

The clerk says
that even with a net
she will not attempt
to catch it.

In an instant
I see what brought me
to this store   I go in
and purchase it

I have always said
"If I could find it"

Now that I have
I carry it home

like glass or love.

　　　*　*　*

Who bought these?
She didn't bring
this package home

She didn't buy
shaving lotion   shingle nails
or breath-mints

The empty wrapping
wrinkles
in her hand

What should she do
with these things?

She can't bring herself
to look at them
or touch them

She meets silence
in the living room
It smells
like shaving lotion.

* * *

At the shopping mall a Boy Scout
sells Jan a bar of melted chocolate

In the window of the Metropolitan
a coloured light flashes *Two for One*

She looks for tiny glass ornaments
to add to her most recent collection

The clerk thinks the pink sweater
looks lovely with her orange hair

She buys six balloons for her son
who likes to pop them with a pin.

* * *

"There is no fun in anything"
he tells me
Standing like a stick-man
in the hallway

having come out of his office
where natural light is blinding

Photocopiers   desks   notices
of meetings   Secretaries
pass him by
He has grown thin
Smokes instead of eating
Can barely stand by himself

(A curious thing)
No   I do not mean him
this bone broken-branch of nothing
I mean the red line
cutting through the centre
of his silent right eye.

* * *

Remembering how we moved closer together
You moving in your house next to mine
Remembering your inner orange walls
complementing my blue walls
Remembering your framed windows
looking into my framed windows
And mostly remembering the birds
in our chimneys
that died in the first cold spell.

* * *

In the doorway
of the Magic Forest Music store
small birds gather

It is the dark hedge
that bars the music
from going on

Clouds are low
and the shop assistant
plays a Mozart concerto

I try to follow the notes
They reach the sun
and beyond

I move to step inside

Small birds flitter
It is almost noon.

* * *

A lantern swings light
on wet pavement

I break eggs
in a frying pan

The baby laughs:
one white tooth

In a paper sack
Uncle finds a jelly bean

Our neighbour hangs a crystal
in her window.

* * *

You are crying
crying into your hands
that cup your head

I too cry sometimes
when I cry
I cry to talk

You are crying
but I do not touch you
or talk to you

My hands are moist
there are tears
in my hands too.

*   *   *

There are no pockets in this city
large enough to fall into
like a worn dollar bill
There are no holes big enough
to crawl through
like a shabby brown mouse
There are only streets   windows
and Public Gardens
where I walk elbow to elbow
among glass   plastic and flowers
with everyone else.

* * *

Expensive wine and a place to dine
is what she wants
She rings the bell for service
and feels like England's ambassador
when three waiters wait
She measures their height
with two beautiful eyes
and claims shyness

But if they were to turn
and wait on someone else
She'd chain-smoke
tip the bell upside down
and fill it with her ashes
then beat her spoon.

* * *

Getting your children
out of the toy shop
through the concourse
and into the parking lot
seemed to take hours
and perhaps did
But what I remember best
were those seven pairs
of saddle shoes
and seven pairs of arms
wrapped around
seven black and white
stuffed puppies   Other people's
happy face kids suddenly pointing
wanting   wailing   Sorrow everywhere
until your children were
in the back seats
of the station wagon
and we drove away
playing
red light   green light
at every stop.

* * *

I am reading about death
in the park
and a child rides by
astride Daddy's shoulders
clutching his thick neck
stifling his breath.

*   *   *

The owner of this shop
was once my Doctor
but here among the books
will he recall
my childhood   spotted-nakedness
swollen glands   allergies
Cough syrup?
How I screamed
when he pulled my Snoopy shirt
over my head

If I buy a book
will he ask me how I am?
If I reply
will he slip a stick
out of his pocket   trap my tongue
till I confess?
"I still don't brush
regularly"

Does he
hear the creak
of my arthritic knee?
Notice
my thick neck
the shoulders bent round
the weight packed on?

If I can't find a book
will he prescribe one
for me?

* * *

Where is that sound?
Where but from a parakeet
high in its cage
with a price-tag on its wing

How does it tune its voice?
On a wire
How does it sharpen its claws?
On a wooden pipe

All of us looking around
and down
talking to mice and fish
and smaller things

While all the while
it sings
"Look up" "Look up"

* * *

There is poetry in his action
He maneouvers the crane into position
It reaches down and catches
the wire holding
The stack of lumber
is lifted into the air
It bends like branches
The driver swings the crane around
From here he looks like a boy
I like to think that
That is what he is.

* * *

His mother has a face like a bird
She looks almost scared
when he helps her to the seat
They have the Mother's Day Special
He suggests that
She asks for smaller portions

He eats his steak
His white shirt tight
around his thick pink neck
His black hair slicked back
She still chooses his clothes
His pantlegs are too short

They have nothing to talk about
except the food
He asks for chocolate milk
She cannot chew the meat.

* * *

I pass a red ticket
to the sailor
Step across
the crack of water
into the boat
for a cruise
along the harbour

Waves rise
like heads of white birds
The boat sways a little
Enough

Children cry

He pulls the anchor up
We move out into tide water.

* * *

Yesterday I got contact lenses
Today when I wore them to Church   every
letter in the Hymn Book seemed as big
as an offering

When we sang "All Things Bright
and Beautiful"
I sang louder than anyone else

Just this once I sang it for myself

Then when we were to bow our heads
for silent prayer   I felt guilty
and looked to catch the Minister's glance
but his eyes read forgiveness

Now I ask forgiveness again
for when I gave my gift to Christ
I gave three nickels instead of quarters

because they seemed so large.

* * *

I am a consumer of medicare
The Doctor came   and the nurse
this evening

thinks massaging eases pain
thinks five minutes of hands heal
but not even the Doctor knows

night's cut   pain killer given
I lie not quite mesmerized
in breathing dark

one pale consumer of medicare
sucking stale ginger-ale
out of a bent white straw.

* * *

They have closed the doors on the dead
Yet every early morning I see the hearse
pulling away from Emergency   Its headlights
haunting the highway   Traffic moving respectfully
to the right
I look across the city and river
to where the sun blots the sky

I soothe pain with my right hand
and steady the silence with my left

Each morning the nurse comes to wake me.

*   *   *

Sometimes she gets happy
on Demerol or Morphine
and turns this place
into a park

She sits atop white sheets
like a swan on a wave
Even the air conditioning
is music

Sometimes she stands
(and though the sides are up)
steps over the edge
and lets the white gown
loose

And sometimes when
she is really happy
she shouts greetings
to passers-by

But sometimes I see her
lying like a tired bather
on a sun-flooded beach

pressing cotton-batting
to her burning wound.

* * *

They never took pictures
of their daughter
At least not ones
that could be seen
without the eye
of a magnifying glass

But then
why would they have wanted to?
She was always there
Strange   silent
Caught in their barrier
their arms
net around her

The background of all the things
   they gave her
      was seemingless

Their constant finger snapping
left her nervous
as a crayfish
in chilling wind
in water
not smooth enough
for reflection

How to tell them
that sometimes even now
something passes over her
like a glass ship
displaying an image
a coloured shadow
that gestures
violently.

* * *

Summer descends on the city
A sprinkler dampens the driveway
The workman removes our storm windows
and puts up screens

I take the day off
trying to decide
what to do

I imagine driving a Rolls Royce
into the country
the big wheel   my hands at ten and two
everything shaped and clear

This afternoon my silent roommate
lies on the lawn
eating cherry cheese cake
and rubbing lotion
on her arms.

*   *   *

Air Canada has taken my luggage
and left me behind
                      "That's my flight"
I cry   "They're waiting for me there"
As if 'there' is some far planet
and 'They' are all the creatures
I've known

              NEXT FLIGHT 24 HOURS

"But I'm a graduate student"   I scream
as if that will bring them to attention
              make them flag my luggage
out of the tall sky
        They turn away
"I'm a poet"   I screech
            They slam the booth door
What do they expect me to do
Sit here and imagine flying?

"My friends are waiting"   I whimper
and the noun echoes like a sonic boom
in the airport's empty seats.

                    *   *   *

What should I carry
into this day?   It is a rule
All shoppers must carry
something

I will not bind my hands
This is my rule

Whatever I carry
must fit nicely
in the hollow
of my skull.

                     * * *